The Mysteries Of A Virgin's Agony

The Mysteries Of A Virgin's Agony

Love Stories Put Into Poetry

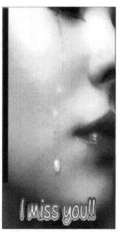

Your Travelling Companion

. . . . d wind walked to the mountain only to find its own heart, walked in its own shadow in love with itself in despair . . . .

Cecilia Naa Densua Quarshie

authorHOUSE®

AuthorHouse™
1663 Liberty Drive
Bloomington, IN 47403
www.authorhouse.com
Phone: 1-800-839-8640

First published by AuthorHouse   08/31/2011

ISBN: 978-1-4567-9718-8 (sc)
ISBN: 978-1-4567-9719-5 (ebk)

Printed in the United States of America

Contents

Preface

This book is intended for all purposes, which include classroom discussion on poetry, and other purposes such as performing poetry, readers own pleasure and so on. Most of the poems have real story lines in them, which are very emotional and should be read as such.

For classroom purposes such as discussions, the writer uses a number of literary terms such as simile, metaphors, irony and in some parts keeps the reader in suspense. Some of the poems are clear and straightforward whereas others are not straightforward. Some get the interest of the reader going as this keeps the reader in suspense and anxious for what follows next.

It is the writers hope that all readers make good use of the book in their own unique ways.

Acknowledgents

I wish to thank Michael Duodu an I.T consultant in the United States for the encouragements he gave me many years ago in coming up with my own poetry book.

The following were very helpful in encouraging my studies in High School to be amongst the best students. Mrs Ako Addo currently the headmistress of Aburi Girls School (Ghana—2011) and Mr Ofori Adjei currently the headmaster of Accra Academy (Ghana—2011). These two have been supportive of my dream since high school. Not forgetting Mirja Villman, English tutor in Laurea University of Applied Sciences (Finland) for her kind support in editing some of the poems.

Kitari Mayele, cultural producer of Caisa Multicultural Centre, Finland, I have not forgotten you, thank you as well for the encouragement and opportunities you always offer me to make me shine. My sincere gratitude to Christfred Anyane and Bryden Nii Laryea Koney (Ghana) for the support and advice given me towards the completion of this book.

Dedication

My first dedication goes to my son and pride Nana Ato—Kwamena Akyer Brainoo and my godfather Emmanuel Boadi, Monitoring and Evaluation Specialist in UNDP.

Other dedication goes to my wonderful mother Nancy Nakuo Kumodzi and to Selorme Azumah (Ghana) for the opportunities given me in developing myself. I love you all.

Contact Information

For bulk, purchases please contact the publisher:

AuthorHouse UK Limited
+44 8001974150

To contact the author please write to
ceciliaghfin@yahoo.co.uk

1. Is It Mine Or Never Before & After

I saw it, I heard it
I felt it, I knew it
I anticipated
Nevertheless, there and then it blew
I thought it was just a dream

A dream never to come true
A dream without hope
A dream of fear and insecurity
That dream came like the rainbow
That dream flew like the birds

It chapped, it tweeted, it whistled
Then I let go
No, it is just a fantasy
This can never be

Softly and tenderly, I let go
Gush!
Ooosh!
Ouch!

Was that a dream?
I see it, I hear it, and I feel it
I know it, It is clear
Hearts beats as of a thunder

Then I held the palm in my paws
The heart spoke through it to my heart
Unsecure, scared but hopeful
It just could not pass by
So strong with passion and aggression, I let go
Mouth to mouth, the bond sparkled
Then the soul paved it way

With peace, with joy, with truth, with reality
It happened, as it had never been
The dream I had hoped for
But never knew it will be
Gush!
Ouch!
Noooh! Noooh! Noooh!

That slenderness had to fade
Is it mine? Is it meant to be?
Is it meant for someone else?
Where is the key to unlock that prison?
Where is the weapon to break the heavy chains?
Chains heavier than weapons
I had to let go
Nature! Thou can tell of tomorrow

2. Adios I Say So Long

What joy! What happiness! What love!
What else can one wish for . . . ?

Those days were days untold of
The moments shared
The joy shared
The pain shared

A friend indeed who can be
A friend indeed who can tell
A friend indeed who can hope for

Those nights of vivacious love glittering
Those nights of reality
Those nights on the strange land

Those words, those lyrics was not to be forgotten
'Are you forcing me to drink of it?
'Anyway a chilled guidance I ask of"
'Anyway a chilled garden I ask for'

That young sunflower with the land so huge around the
waist
Ohh never knew she was that young

She served in the garden; she served the guidance to make
profit

As I walk away, they yelled with innocence, fear and said:
'Are you leaving the pot of treasure?
An alien may come for it
With naïveté I turned and laughed

Was it just words of the now?
Was it just words of the future?
In bed I laid and on the wonderland I walked

Who can tell?
Ohhh yes, I remember
'Dont look at Allah' was the words
And the story untold of

Off we go,
Off we depart
Adios my love
Au revoir mon amour
Goodbye I say

So long, so long, So long
Let life be So long hailed the future

3. How Do I Sleep

How do I sleep, when all I hear of is your heartbeat?
How do I sleep when it just cannot seem to fade away?
How do I sleep when the thunders keep talking so high and
the babes cease to continue their sleep?
How do I sleep when all I see is your face?
How do I sleep when my thirst cannot be satisfied?
How do I sleep when it just cannot seem to go away?
How do I sleep?

That innocent face was untold of with its held up speech
It was that day that I saw that story that was to be told soon

That sparkle in your eye gave me so much hope
That sparkle in your eye spoke to me of the future

That sparkle in your eye told me the thunder was for a
season
That sparkle in your eye told me to dream of yesterday
That sparkle in your eye told me not to lose hope

That sparkle 'sparkled' the future of awesomeness into my
bosom
That sparkle brought joy into the unknown heart

How do I sleep when I just cannot let go
How do I sleep when all I can see, is your face
How do I sleep when the hands cannot just stop encrypting?
How do I sleep when the confusion cannot just turn to
emotion?

*How do I sleep when the hopes of tomorrow seems to fade
into hopes of yesterday
How do I sleep when all I feel is the warmth of your
embrace?
How do I sleep when all I can hear is voices of the birds
chipping your name?*

*I wish I could answer those questions with so much vague
meanings
I wish I could see into the future
I wish I could tell of tomorrow and its hopes
I wish I could tell of yesterday and its disappointments
I wish I never saw that dream come true
I wish I never dreamt of such a dream
I wish I never saw those sparkles
I wish it never came forth*

4. How Do I Forget You

With one teardrop,
I remembered the beginning to the end
That drop of tear opened

5. My Heart Was Opened

I am bleeding so profusely and it cannot seem to stop
I am bleeding so much that I cannot bear it anymore
My heart is bleeding with thunders from above
It is bleeding so much with storms and the waves unheard of
My heart is bleeding of so much listening as if there is no
tomorrow

I gave you my heart
My heart was opened to you
I gave you my life in my heart
I gave you my words
I gave you my soul

My heart is bleeding so much that I cannot bear it anymore

How do you doubt it when I opened my heart to you?
How do you doubt me, when I gave you the knife to pierce
my heart?

How do you doubt me, when all I told you was all I was?
My heart is bleeding so much because it is fainting and
getting weary

*If I knew what was in your heart, I would not have opened
all my heart*
*If I knew what was in your heart, I would not have opened
my eyes*
*If I knew what was in your heart, I will not have opened my
entire mind*
If I knew what was in your heart, I would not have said it all
*If I only knew what I did not know, my heart would have
ceased to open*

You became the life my heart was looking for
*And you became the salvation of the lost soul searching for
its home*
All I saw in you, was the hope of my fate
*Never did I know my heart was falling into the wrong
tunnel of lost hopes with doubts . . . . If only I could tell the
future . . . .*

*Why do you have to doubt me, when all you know is my
heart?*
Why do you have to doubt me when all you know is my life?
*Why do you have to doubt me when all I know is being
genuine with you?*
*Why do you have to doubt me when I told you, you were all
I had*
Did you have to doubt me?
I thought you were the lost world I was looking for
*Why didn't I question it all to be sure, you were the lost
world?*
*How could I not have seen of tomorrow and its untold
stories?*
It broke my heart into drops when I realised you had doubts
*How can a genuine heart be so true when no one sees how
true it is?*

6. Why Did I

It looked so pleasant and appealing from afar
It looked so trustful and blissful from behind
The waves thereof were like the peace one has never hoped for

Why did I cross the river was a question that never came forth
Its waters were so blue and faithful when I went near
It brought so much strength when I saw how it waved all over
It brought me so much peace as I watched from afar
It was a river, a river, a river of hopes without fear

Why did I cross the river was a question that never came forth

Did I see it coming?
Did I see that wave of uncertainty?
Did I see what I never expected?

Why did I cross the river was a question that never came forth

How will I know if that river was just a camouflage?
How will I know if that river was there for nature with a
purpose?
How will I know if that river was a land but my eyes
deceived me?

Why did I cross the river was a question that never came forth
I never saw it coming with such a strong wave
The storm of it was so silent I could not tell

If only I knew of yesterday, tomorrow would not have been
a puzzle

7. Was It A Game

Was it love or was it a game
Why did you call me uninvited when you knew it was a game
Why did I call you to be invited when I did not know it was
to be played?

I thought it was nature's own will for us to meet
I thought we were destined to be in that land
A land so pure
A land so true
A land so honest
A land so deep
A land so rich
A land that was to be harvested

Why did you regret it?
Why did you wish it never were?
Why did you have to ask 'why you'

Never did I regret it
Never did I plan to regret of it
Nor did nature tell me to regret of it

It was my life and the life I had longed for
It was a true life with natural life in it
I thought it was meant to be

Yes it was meant to be, that was what I heard from the birds
Even the wind whistled it out although its voice was fading
The land was ready to be harvested

The road looked impossible and awkward
The road was rough and ugly
The road was unpleasant and had no hope

Nevertheless, I had hope for the waters
I knew the water would settle in its due time
I knew the waters would gather where it was destined to be

Was it the same Spirit of hope you had from the onset?
Was it the same Power of strength that you held on to?
Was it the same faith and armour you had?

How could I tell now when all seems unclear
How can I tell now, when the wind is blowing so hard, and
the dust fleeing to a land unknown?
How do I tell of tomorrow when today cannot seem to know
its existence

A game it could be who can tell

8. Never Will I Know

Never did I know it would end like this
I cherished every moment of our friendship
I cherished every moment we spent together
I could not ask for more than what we had
I could not thirst for more than what we shared
I could not hunger for more because there was no need to

I thought it was meant to be
There was life in the tunnel, a tunnel so true of real
friendship
Yes, that was a dream I never dreamt of

A friend so true, who can find
A friend so real, who can have
A friend so loving, who can be weary of?
That friend was more than a friend
That friend became to me as my part
That friend became to me a life of hope and reality
I could not ask for more than what we had
I could not thirst for more than what we shared
I could not hunger for more because there was no need to

9. The Dance

There it was the song that was sang to the hearing of the natives
They danced to the music but the players stop playing the
rhythm
Moreover, there was no rhythm for the dancers but they did
dance anyway

She saw him from afar and felt he was the one
He adhered to the music and followed the pitch
Ready or not ready, she knew not from the thoughts of him
and from his heart

Here he came with vigorous hope and despair
Was he confused with hope but with determination? Who
could tell?

Unveiling she became when he danced to her
Stunned he became as he was left helpless
Was she ready or in for a game? Rhetoric question for him

Was she paranoid or did not plan of it, he asked the beaters
of the drums

He left her on the dancing floor to live in her paranoiac state
She cried and held onto him to depart not but alas, he flew

She saw a bunch of them, flowers made of love and hope
To his dancing room, it was taken
What he thought of it, she knew not of the beats it could give
to the music
Was it the right or wrong instrument, she could not tell of
the band
Than to wait if, a melody could come out of the music

Then they met on the stage, finally to play a duet
Her heart was beating as of a roaring sea and horses on a race
All that was needed was a joint melody to make the song
Outrageous as it seemeth, she forgot the lyrics of her own
composition
He still had hope and tried to compose a new song from her song
Where his lyrics in a different language or had a different
connotation
He started to sing with a voice that was from deep within

Horrified as she stood in her paranoiac state, she heard no
music being played
On the floor he kowtowed to her: will you be the Eve of my
offspring
It came like a whirlwind and howled in her presence
She got stunned and felt it was a tale from the wonderland
Did she expect it or was she just a man made clown he
thought in despair
Then he took out all his identities, licence for life, and handed
them to her saying
'Hold these and report to the armies if I sing the wrong
melody to break thy soul'
Was it a drama or a movie she asked herself in her hypnoses state

Back home she strutted with fear and tears
What could have become of the melody if the lyrics were
tuned to the rhythm she asked herself?
Adios, he said to her as he parted away with the camel
It was an adios forever that may or may not see tomorrow
Hardly did she know that adios could split the known music
in the village
Adios, she said back with shame
All she could do was to cry like a child over a love she missed
at the dancing floor

10. Season's Greeting

The years have gone and the months have come
The months came and the days are near
The days arrived and the hours are nigh
The hours are waiting and the second's ticks

The season never remain the same
The moments keep changing
Times never remain the same
So has the periods been like

Your unsparing love has been my glow
Nothing I ever wish to have more
Your heart has shown enough care and love

All I beseech of thee is to keep it safe and whole

Falling in love with you is like a new leaf out of my hope

Giving you up is no more a wish I pray for

You will always remain the love of my life
Just hold me close to thy heart every moment

May this season never pass us by without a memory
May our hearts unite in perfect harmony
May the season continue to fill our hearts with joy and love

11. I Saw Not

Did I see it coming?
Is a question uncalled for
Did you planned it coming
Is a dollar question for the contest?

Never did I know love could be like red wine
Details of it cannot be apprehended
Illusion was all I could put in my paranoiac state
Out of defence and pretence, I had to let go
But, the thoughts of it alone raced my heart on the road
Alas, I brought out the cat from the wardrobe

Risky is the journey
Mad love it is called

That is a paranoiac journey
Risky it can be

Nay I cannot keep holding on my true feelings
Deterioration was all I anticipated as I hide in the corner
I could not keep hiding in the prison
Overflowing pattern of love I let go off
Bright and hopeful it looked for the future
Altitude was the hope for the risky journey

Risky is the journey
Mad love it is called
That is a paranoiac journey
Risky it can be
As I lay in bed, thoughts of you ceased my sleep
All I could do was to think of you
My heart beat as of a thunder at every glance I make
memory of
What could this be?
What could be its future?

Nothing was to be lost or not expected
All you will have is my heart
Anything you will need is at your expense
Do not live that loneliness anymore
Eagle I am, am here to soothe your loneliness
Nadia lay your head on my shoulder with passion
Surely, nothing will set us apart as I hope for
Unsure as it may look
All I hope for is a brighter future for us

Risky is the journey
Mad love it is called
That is a paranoiac journey
Risky it can be

12. The Answer I Find Not

How it happened I could not tell
How could this be another hard journey again?
Why did you start when you knew you could not complete
it?
Why did you open the seal when you knew you could not
close it again?

I thought it was a new fresh start
I thought it was meant to be
How could it be one of the stories to tell again?
Why didn't I see it at the start that it was for a while?

If I had read the pages, well and had seen its mystery well
I would not have given in with all my heart

If I had seen the desert behind the deep blue sea, I would
have gone for a camel
But the ship got stuck at the shore and I had nothing to
travel on to continue my journey

All I did was to sit with no plan until all got rotten and
faded away

13. You Walked Away

I thought falling in love was no more a dish of mine to eat
How could I sell my heart indefinitely to a city that was full
of aliens I will never get used to?
Your love kept me going
You love made me see the brighter side of life
Nothing I felt could have been as good as this love
Buried in your heart was my love
How could it have happened this way?
It was my choice to fall that deep with your heart
But here I am all have changed for the worse

You walked away without saying anything
You walked away without a goodbye
You walked away without telling me where I went wrong

You walked away without telling me your past had gone
well for you
You walked away without making me get out of it with
reason
You walked away without a kiss
You walked away without knowing who I was
You walked away without seeing eye to eye for the last time
You walked away and left my heart torn apart
All I saw was your shadow leaving without a message to me
But I could not see the message on the face that left
It left me confuse forever
It left me in a pool of tears with all the beauty I saw in it

14. How I Thought

How could you do this to me?
How could you hurt me this deep when you knew my
sorrows?
How could you have torn my heart into pieces when you
were all the joy I had?
How could you have pretended I was special to you when
you knew it was for a moment?
How could I have allowed this to happen to me again?

I swore in my heart never to fall this deep ever
But how could I have gone beyond the tunnel when I had
seen the pain in it
How could I have travelled the mile I promised never ever to
cross again?

How could I have pierced my heart with the knife in my hands?
If I had seen this coming, I will have not committed this deep

I thought we were meant to be

I thought we were compatible with all we had in common
I thought we had dreams of laughter and dreams of joy
I thought we could be in each other's arms forever
I thought we were there to share our pains and cover it in time

But never did I know it was all for a moment
Everything that happened was just a story from one of the
fairies
It was from a wonderland that had nothing in existence
I was not paranoid but it was all with Mary on wonderland
Nothing was ever true; all were just tales from the
wilderness

15. It Was Just A Dream

Sobbing all night and day was never the answer
The tears could never make it up to a river
A river that could be travelled on to go to where I lost my heart
There was no boat either to use in sailing on the river
A wild dream I had but nothing I could do to bring it back
Except to keep crying until I get over it

I thought I could let go before the new season
I tried to be strong on it and told myself I had won the battle
of fear and tears
I got into the new season feeling empowered with new hopes
to see the brighter side of life

But here I am wailing again without control
Was it the right time to say goodbye
Going our separate ways was never the right time to do that

16. It Came To Pass

And it came to pass

And it came to pass
Because they believed, it will come to pass

Was it a miracle?
They could not believe it came to pass
That desire finally came to pass

And it came to pass
As they strutted back home with joy
Who knew it would have come to pass
With joy, love and peace, they looked at each other

It indeed came to pass

At long last, it did happen
It was a dream come true
A dream that looked impossible those days

A dream that made the whole world to stare at them

Who knew this dream would have been a reality
A dream with love but with uncertainty
It finally happened with a blessing
The road had been challenging
But they each did not lose hope
Because they were determined to make it come true

What joy can one wish for? . . . . 'The days ahead
The memories to leave . . . . The moments to share
The thought of a loved one close by you each day
The feeling of someone you can lean your life on
A trust of whom you can dedicate your life to'
It came to pass as they had wished and dreamt of
The joy and the feeling of seeing it come to pass cannot be fathom
Words could not tell what their hearts were singing
They did pray for it to come to pass
But it came to pass with more joy and happiness
As the four legged operator drove them to their place of abode
Tears was shared on what the Maker had finally done for them
Because it was a dream come true
As she rested on his chest
With tears of joy dropping from within
He held her hands with passion with his paw
And told her
'I meant those words I spoke to you because they were from
my heart'
A dream come true, who will not adore it
The Maker finally blessed them and gave them the way ahead
The way to their land of joy in Canaan finally came to pass
The dream came through as they had wished for

Then they got home
The moment of seeing that dream come through was still a
miracle to her
She could not help the tears of joy
She could not believe that dream had finally come to pass
A dream they say can come to pass if you believe—she told herself
At long last, their true love dream came to pass
What will be the story of tomorrow?
All they prayed for was the guidance from the Almighty one
To let His peace and favour be sovereign in their lives
True love they say, truly exists . . . .

17. At Last

At last, it happened
At last, I found the lost coin
At last, I lost the coin
At last, that moment came
At last, its season arrived

As I walked through the thick
As I walked through the thorns
As the days showed of no hope
As the moments, faded away
As the stars dimness arrived

All I could see was no hope
All I could hear was no love
All I could see was pain
All I could see was a lost hope
All I could see was blindness

A touch of hope, I dreamt of

A time of faith, I died for
A time of it own . . . . I cried

A time with lost treasures
A time when no one saw me

Again, that phase passed by
Again, that love embraced me
Again, that faith came back
Again, that moment arrived
Again, I knew it was time

At last, I said it again
At last, I was determined
At last, I saw it coming
At last, it was all not lost
At last, I was assured again
Yes at last all I wanted rained
The journey had been of pain
The journey had been of thirst and hunger

18. At Last (Part 2)

There were times I needed water to assuage my thirst
Nevertheless, none I could find to help me

I saw them laugh
I saw them mock
I saw them whisper to each other
I saw that excitement on their faces because I lost it all

Then I found it, yes I found that coin I had longed for
I gave it my full commitment
It was what was ordained of an eve
I was determined to complete the journey

I sacrificed for the coin and its entourage forgetting my own
world

However, nay, from the beginning, that coin just showed off
its nature
I thought I could change that coin
I thought I could make it my own coin

I thought as I thought
But no, all my endeavours
Was taken for a fool
I tried to prove I was not a fool but only a dedicated eve
But nothing I did was appreciated
All that coin did was to please his desire with foreign coins
of its own kind

It was not my coin . . . .
Then the story continued with pain as it was narrated
Did I say at last?
Did something arrive again?

No, I did not see it coming
The friendship was built
The trust was to be fulfilled
The hope of a hope was due

19. At Last (Part 3)

And I found my eye
My lost eye at last I found
'My love', he said
I was convinced he was the one
I was convinced he was the one
I was convinced he was the one
I knew he was the one
I knew he was the one

Where was he all this while, I wept
Where was he when I needed him, all this while?
Why didn't we meet that early

Why did it have to happen this way?
Why did it have to be this way?

Yes, I welcomed my eye

I embraced my eye
And I put my eye where it belonged
And I slept so sweet with my eye back to it place

Then I dreamt of a treasure land

Then I woke up to the garden
I walked through that garden
And I was fullness of joy
Joy that no one could explain
Joy that was there forever
Joy that no one will understand

Oh No! Oh No! Oh No!
My vision became impaired
Then I stumbled and fell on the leaves
Then I crawled to the river
And I washed my face
The eye fell into the water
As I looked at the eye
I saw there was another eye in it
I took it and watched it well
But there was another eye
I wept until the river got overflowed..I wept and wept and
wept

20. At Last (Part4)

Why me, why me again
Why me, was it meant to be so
The eye just fitted so well
It was just like my eye
But this eye had a eye in it

Therefore, I took the risk
A risk that was hard to take
It was difficult to swallow
But I decided to do it
A risk I was scared of the outcome
Yes, I was full of fear

I was scared if I tell the eye:
' We have to wait' the eye will go to bed forever and never
come to see me again
I was full of fear, the eye will just bade me goodbye
However, I assured myself, if that eye were mine, it would be

Then the eye spoke
I thought it was going to look
For me to tell what I see
But the eye talked
It was a miracle
The eye was not dumb
The eye had a mouth
I wanted to shout with joy
I wanted to tell the whole world
The eye just talked to me
The eye was not just watching

But the eye could talk
It had a voice
The eye, yes has a voice
The eye told me,

I'm dumbfounded but can't blame you for anything
That notwithstanding I'm still seeing after the Hamatan!
The humour still lives

21. At Last (Part 5)

I laughed and cried
I laughed so loud and cried so loud
I laughed so loud with hope and trust
I laughed and cried as though it was time to tie the knot
before the crowd
I fell that moment
I could not stop crying
I wish I could have . . . . to my eye
Then at that moment, I heard that voice:
That is the eye I ordained

Oh, that still small voice spoke it
Then I stopped crying
It was as though a burden was lifted
It felt like; this was my day of restoration

I was energised once more after many years of being dead within
I felt that power again from above
That hope came again
It was just like when I first found my saviour
Then I screamed and told Him
'Let they will and only thy will be done'

Then for a moment, I felt they were around me
I felt those Holy ones singing with me
At last, I was determined and was full of hope; my eye will
be my eye in its due time
And am not going to share my eye with no other eye
Then I began to sing
My lips could not just stop singing as the words proceeded

'I sing because am happy,
I sing because am free
His eyes is on the Sparrow
And he watches over me'

At last, it happened
At last, the confidence I lost many years ago redefined itself
into reality¨
I was full of confidence, that eye is meant to be mine
I was not scared of its return
Because I knew, Yaweh will bring me my eye in its due time

What joy, what peace, what peace, what hope can one ever
wish for
In hundred and twenty-four days, am going to see my eye
That will tell more of tomorrow
124, is just a number and will soon pass by I told myself
All I pray for, is to see no eye in my eye in its due time
because now I believe that eye is mine
I pray am convinced with the right message that, that eye is
my eye to be

How I wish I could convey how I feel in words and action
But one thing I know for sure
The season will come to pass
All I need is patience
That is the virtue
That time, that season, that moment, that period shall come
The sun shall shine again !!!!!!!!

22. Dont Get Lost

Loosing you is not going to be what I will stand for
I do not want to mislay you
I have fallen in love with you so much that I cannot help it
Confuse I make myself sometimes, scared I make myself
sometimes
Doubtful I make myself sometimes, but not anymore
I am hopeful now, and more determine

I want to be in thy bosom each night
I want to hold you forever
I want to see you every moment
I want to touch you every minute
I want to look in your eyes and tell you how much I love you

It does not matter anymore who you are
Because I do trust you with my life and all I am
With a positive hope that you are genuine and truthful

I love you with every bit of my heart

Please stay close to my heart and never part away
Please hold it close to thy heart so I feel each heart beat of yours
Please hold it safely to yours and do not let it die of thirst
Please do not tear it apart because it is fragile
Please let it be in thy heart because I love you truly
Please do not let me part from you no matter what

I cannot stop loving you and please do let me beg for it
I cannot stop thinking about you
I cannot take you out of my heart
I could not walk but have fallen in love with you
I will not know how to wake up from it if I have to

Please hold me dear to thy heart
Because you are all I have now in my heart
I love you and I will always love you
Please cherish me in your life because I do cherish you very much
Every teardrop that comes now is of hope and love
Now I am not scared of trusting and loving you
Nevertheless, I am scared to lose you
The Maker knows my heart; you are the one in my heart
now
I will never give up on you
Am going to fight if that is what I have to do to win your heart

23. Flaw Or Right

Why lay me in bed
Sobbing in bed
With no purpose
And with purpose
Is there an answer
Can I answer?
It is my reason

Why did I drive?
When I knew
It is not my wheel

How I feel
Is of lunatic
If I knew it today

It started all nicely
Unplanned was it

Not to recall it
The times shared
The sweet moment
All was unique

What was wrong?
Did it go wrong?
Is it wrong again?

Did I reflect?
Did I learn?
Did I plan?

If only I knew
If only I could see
If only it was one

I feel broken inside
I want to hide
It is hectic, the journey it is

24. Flaw Or Right (Part 2)

Why sob more
Why weep more
Why cry much

Is it my instincts?
Or my intuition
Or is it a knack

I can feel the rope
It is untying
The knob fainted

Did I push hard?
Am I pushing?
Is it too much

I feel broken inside
I cannot admit
It is hard to say

Why ' I ' go deeper
When it's not mine

When it can fall
Why torment it
Why break it
Why unveil it

I err again
I felt the eeriest
Did I listen?

How I missed
The moments
It is sparkling
Full of Grace

Why weep again
When I can see
It may not be mine
It happened again
My weakness . . . . My flaw it is

25. Flaw Or Right (Part3)

Why fall deep
Why break out
Why not tarry

Am sorry
If I blame you
And it hurts you

I feel broken inside
Because I miss you
Am I wrong again?

Wish to look
Deep in your eyes
And you do same

Do I have a day?
To tell you again
How much I miss

I hurt myself
For hurting you
It happened again
Am I right to say
That it has change
Yesterday changed

I promised myself
That was the last
Never to repeat

Why go so deep
When I knew not
Why hurt myself

With no promise
I kept digging
With no plan

Why fall I
Why go I
This deep a journey
My flaw again
Blemish it looked
Where I can't hide

26. Flaw Or Right (Part 4)

Is it fading?
I see it evaporating
The loss vanishing

It is hard to say
Will you tell me?
If I am wrong

Was it a moment?
Sharing for a while
I try to bid for it

Is it a silent one?
A message to read
I hate to read it

I did not read it
I did not anticipate
If I knew, it was

Why set the rule
And break my rule
Why do it again
I feel broke inside
With the changes
Slow but true

Though with doubt
Though with fear
Though with truth

I travelled deep
Without walking in
I fell in it

I told them to walk
Falling is a risk
You may never rise
Here I break it: A rule I made: I could not obey

27. Flaw Or Right (Part5)

So deep, I see
The milk spilled
It divulged all over

Is it a message?
A silent message
Created for me

Why fall in a pit
I dig not
And knew not

How I missed all
How I missed it
How I missed that

Am I paranoid?
By the silent voice
The silent message

As easy as I said
I will laugh of it

And joy with it
If it's never mine
If it fades away

And becomes one
One of the stories
Stories and lessons
Can I laugh and joy

But never forget 'I'
That I pushed it
It was a quick nod
I waggled through
Just too early

Confused as I lay
I cry to sleep
To dream not

But to sleep
Sleep forever
And tarry no more
And hope no more
And dream not

Never will it be mine
It was not mine
I cannot tell

If the change,
If the silence,
Is of a message

I adhere

28. He Wants Her

(Nonsense poem)

He told himself, i have found the one
She is the apple of my eye
She is the one i had always longed for
Yes she is the one
The sparkling to my life

How best is she from the dame
What if you end up being two clowns
What if you love too much and can't stop

What if she becomes mrs bean
What if you wake up one day only to find she has no tooth

What if you sleep at night only to hear a snore like horses running

What if you see her stand on the toilet instead of sitting
What if she uses the bath tab to store drinking water

Love they say is a crazy world
Have you thought? What if she belches like a bomb
After eating
What if she farts so bad all the flowers in the house dies

Are you sure, you want a comedian
Hope your kids do not become clowns as well

On your wedding day, she will appear with diapers,
brassieres & winter boots

29. Isn't It?

Is it all right but it is all not wrong
Is it all wrong but it is not all right
I like you for who you are
I like you for how you look
I love your company
I love you for who you are made of
Do I know you as I think?
Is it a question for the contest?
I love your smile
Is it a time for a while?
Is it for now and never ever?

The light in the sun is dimming away
My needs are stuck on the road
Is it ok if it happens unplanned?
Is it ok for me to dream of us making love?
It did happen I saw it and felt it

Is it ok for me to see you as mine?

It may be wrong if we start on the road
It may be wrong if we do not start the journey
It may be wrong if we give up
It may be wrong if we do not give up
It may be wrong if we remain true

It may be wrong if we become infidel

Is it all wrong but it is all right?

Do I now need someone so bad?
Is it going to last forever?

Close your eyes
As I speak to your heart
Am I yours?
Are your needs for me?
Will you ever be there when I need you?
Will it ever be us?
Am I asking too much?
Will the sun that shines comes alive again
I miss you
It may not seem that way
But I do

Am I taking what does not belong to me?
A question I need an answer for
Why this continuous feeling with no faith and fear

30. Can You

Can you see it from afar?
My heart is breaking just for you
My arms are open just for you
Was there an illusion, which I cannot tell?
Nevertheless, I know my heart is stored for you
Those hidden tears are just for you
Those tears need you protection to keep me stronger

31. Kiss

Give me a kiss he made his plight known
Proud I felt, was flattered to share my love
The look on his face told me of a hope of a day to come
That kiss came from a true heart to him

The kiss of pride and plied
The kiss of joy and pride
The kiss of plied and joy
Was it a fey, nay it was real

The wishes kept heaping

Wish I could touch him
Wish I could feel that soft skin on his cheek

Wish I could hold those soft hands in the paws
Wish I could feel that tenderness
Wish that serene never remains a dream

Gush! Gush! Gush! That heart beat as of a war

Oh, I wish it were soon to come
I that tenderness on his lips
I wish my tongue would touch that tongue

Moreover, see how the wish will take me to dizzy land

32. Is My Friend Lost For A Luv?

After many days, many hours, many minutes, many
seconds, many weeks, many months, many years and ago
We came into contact again
I kept searching and searching from him through the page
I did not find him
Oh Yes! Then he got my contact from him
That king that left those times to the shore
Was he a king? nay the writer just exaggerated?

He became like a brother to her
She genuinely loved him like a brother
He was indeed like a brother to her
He counselled her and was much interested in her safety
She shared any piece with him with trust and love

She took any given counsel that came from those lips

How did this happen
Who can tell?
She never dreamt of that to come
She just loved him like a brother she thought
But alas!

He asked, are you the one
Then her heart bleated so fast like never before
What could this be, she asked herself
It happened with no given reason
Was that love there hiding in its abode?

It was neither an act nor pretence.
She felt it as a real life situation
That night before, was a brainstorming of whether it was lust
Nevertheless, when he asked—are you the one?
She felt that true feeling
Why did this feeling never show forth
She always saw him like a brother she loved
But, that was not the story of the book
It was a genuine and true feeling she felt

Selflessness she said 'NO' to it
What wrong has the rose done to him?
He cannot let her go in tears because of you, she told herself
They were in their world before you arrived
Love it is said, wishes for happiness and sacrificing

She spoke in her heart for him to hear
"Let your Rose be, because you may never know
Not let any anger cause any sudden decision because of me
Be patient and give it all you best to see how best your best
can prove its natural aim
Let that protection and security she wants always be there
to keep her strong
If we are meant to be, 'Believe' she said with faith
It will happen in its own way
She hoped he understands the silence message she gives"

Has she lost the friendship for love?
She hoped not, because she cherished the friendship
She cannot take that position because there was a dame there

Without hurt or sadness, she was still joyful
Because they got much hours to spend as friends
Love they say, is an ironic iron that may burn or iron out
As she smiles whilst writing
She said to herself
Am happy the hidden feeling has exploded in its due time

33. Miss You

Is not a game, but from a genuine heart?
I cannot play the puzzle if yours is to be a game
A game they call it, I cannot stand
A game it is but not to be said
A game I refuse and never to see
It is genuine and it hopes to see into that genuine heart

34. Is It All Lost?

That was what was said about it
Two funny naughty mice was what they were known for
Attractive, tiny, smart and easily got adaptable with . . .

What was to be the unknown plight about their future?
To be ? or not to be?
Who could tell?

What was to be the unknown keeps belonging to them?
To have? Or not to have?
What could it be?

What was to be the unknown key to open the heart of that
treasure?
To search? Or not to search?
They both did not see

Alas he told her !
That letter was of a scroll with the Holy words!
'Damn ! He said to himself—
Were thou of love or of the Holy scroll?
This indeed has no story to tell, he affirmed to himself.

CECILIA NAA DENSUA QUARSHIE

That was a decade and silver age ago
Was she thinking of me, during the lost moments?
How does she know that I can see her soul and want see it more
What story could this be of?
What is the unknown mystery to be unfolded?

Confuse as I lay, my mind told me there may be hope

35. That Eye

That eye was like that eye
From a distance, I looked into that eye
That eye that was full of a deep sorrowed message
That eye that was full of passion and peace
That eye that was full of grace and glace
That eye that was full of uncertainty with hope
I saw that eye

It shivered my heart, as I looked into that eye
What was the story behind that eye?
The eye that made me search my soul
Centuries have passed but that eye was full of puzzles

I felt that peace, when I looked into that eye
I felt the passion as I looked into that eye
I felt the future as I looked into that eye
I felt the hopeful journey as I looked into that eye
All I felt was the 'felt' the eye 'felt'

That eye was of a deep message
That eye made to want fly to him

That eye confused my soul as it searched deep in the pit
That eye told me, you may never know
Only that eye could tell of what it needed

You are the eye
You are the eye that can search from within
You are the eye that can tell of tomorrow
You are the eye that can tell if it is possibility
You are the eye that can pave the way
Only that eye can tell of tomorrow

36. Are You The One!

Did I see 'the one' coming?
Nay I could not tell
The laughter, the friendship
The humour, the passion
The stories, the jokes
The memories, the songs
The time—shared, the moments spent
Was it going to be a waste?

She lay in bed and the mind travelled to Canaan
What was it to be of that land?
Was it not honey and bread?
What did the 'Holy Scroll' say?
My mind was lost . . .
Ahoy! Ahoy! Ahoy!
The mind sailed to the ocean
'Then she asked herself—
What will be of its story, if she falls into the dungeon?
Could it affect the friendship? Was a scary question for her.
She told her—'Nay, hold thy state and let nature decide'

Are you the one?
Oh, he did ask
She did not see this coming
Uncertain as she felt, the feeling became reciprocal

When was the first time you had this question, she asked
'This is the first time'
As she went into trance, there is a limited choice

Never say never, she said with love
Let's see how nature turns it way
Take the ship you are sailing safely through the shore

37. That Land Of Sorrow Or Hope

Why give it I a name when I have not gone to the land
Why feel this way when the time has not yet come
Why made I that hope, when it doesn't look that way

I was searching for it
Searching deep for it, could not find it
The sand had heaped all over
Nevertheless, I kept searching for that needle
Although it looked impossible and hopeless
I dedicated to keep searching for that needle

There he comes
Alomo was the name
How was it formed, was a question to be answered
Was he an alomo? Nay he wasn't
Why that name, when he wasn't

I told him of the needle I was in search of
Of the story within and it's empty hope
Hey! Hey! My Goodness! My Goodness!
I could not believe it

He said am gonna make you come
I want to see you
Suddenly I forgot all about the needle

Joy cribbed me in my closet
As I lay softly on it
After the autumn, that dream will come to pass

Never say never as it always go
I pray that land becomes of joy but no sorrow

38. Can That Be?

As they both laid in their abodes
Thought of it kept flashing their minds
Can it be? Can it be?

How will life be, with us together?
How sweet it looks from afar.
Two happy cockroaches with sense and no sense

How will it feel like?
Seeing that happy accomplice in crime each morning
How will it feel like?
Coming from work to see the blissful love from her or him

Can it be? No one could tell
How true can it look from afar?
Such a partner they had both wished for
Creative, crazy and full of humour

It had been difficult with the past treasures
Sometimes joking alone just brings the world war one
Why can't people just understand it is just a 'joke?'

Oh how I wish, there were together

Was the passion of the two souls from within?
'J'taime' was what that soul wrote
'J'taime grand' was the reply of the soul mate if it were
Did they mean it? Or were just passing jokes again

'Who can tell if it can be?
Minä sinun rakastan', it was announced
She said it from deep her true soul
Can it be or can it be not . . . .

39. The Battle

The story was shared to them of a true love yet to cometh
They believeveth in true love but from whence they kneweth
nothing of it
It cameth to pass when they least expected
She met him after the story was untold
He was just what was told of
The non—ending story of love, passion, honesty, respect,
humility and the hand of the Maker in the centre
Who will have believeth if he told of the story himself?
It was like the tale written in scrolls that was just to be narrated
Alas, he was able to share his story to them
All I seeketh is thy love to keep me alive

All I beseech is the true vine in thy heart
All I sought for, is an unfailing love that draweth from
within thine heart
All I ask of thou is thy faithfulness untill death part us away

My heart is what I offer to thee
All you have to doeth is keep it close to life because it may
die if you do not water it

Your lips sparkleth like the stars that shineth from above
That lips speaketh of truth and love
It sayeth unto me soul, : I am the chosen one for thy lost soul
All you will have is my true love that floweth from within my soul
My life I dedicate unto thee
Let it remain as you found it—as you keep it to shine more in
the darkness

True love is what we have seen from deep our hearts
It tells of the new hope for the morrow
The love that sparkleth from deep within
You will always remain my angel and true love sent from Him

Together we shall fight the battle ahead with true love
Together we shall strengthen each other in the journey
Together we shall remain in unity unto our descendants

My heart I have offered unto you with humility
Hold it dear to your heart and it will remain yours forever
These I offer to you accept it and let my heart rest

My heart beateth like the thunder as I saw you offering me
your heart
It told me of how precious my life was to you, in thy life
Indeed my heart raceth as of the horses on the battle road
In their sight you finally offered it to me
In their sight i do promise to keep and uphold it close to mine
Rain or shine, dry or wet, I am thee till thy wanteth no more

You are the treasure I seek for and I will always love you

40. Two Little Thieves

Two little thieves
Looking so innocent
But planning a heavy deal
Who goes first to the bank to do the robbery?
Is the big question in their minds?
No double—crossing, they both contemplated
Else, trouble for someone's— . . . .

41. Letter To My Love

Too anxious I suspected when I saw the damsel.
All she could do was to keep her identity in suspense with little help.
My love, where art thou, she asked the lad who visited her in her dream.
I cannot wait to see eye to eye again with my love she told the lad as he sat by her in tears.

—My love I once missed, she told the lad. A taste of our heart we shared not—

—Worry not the lad soothes her with kindness. Thy love am sure await thee in joy he told her with a soft voice—
She jumped with joy after hearing the prophesy from the lad.
I just cannot wait to see my love again; she went running in the garden with laughter.

How she had dreams' of sharing memorial moments with the love of her heart.

She walked on the flowers talking with the wind as it blew constantly around her making her apparel fly in love.

—It will be eye to eye—
—It will be sincere from our hearts—
—It will be hand in hand—
—Lying on his chest till I fly with the angels—

—*Feel his compassionate hand around me as I listen to his soft love song—*
—*Touch those innocent lips from the genesis—*

I cannot wait any more, she screamed to the flying wind.

In response the birds, the wind, the trees, the rocks, the animals, all that went into the 'ark' told her: tarry not and be anxious for nothing any longer, for thy love is resting in the haven and that is where you both shall be until you want no more.

42. A Dream

All I can see is a bright future as I looked beyond..
The music at the dancing floor was meant for trueness
That was a song never to be forgotten

The lyrics of the music became a mystery to me
As I was stuck on the stage, forgetting my own composed song
She looked like an angel from afar
The beauty in her eyes was like the unknown paradise

The dancers got confuse, as there was no music to be played¨
The singer, here I was dumbfounded by what I saw
Oh my! What was happening to me I could not fathom
Risky it is called, mad love I found in my heart

Dreaming to hold her in my arms was what I kept hoping
Shattered with despair I prayed she could hear the drums in
my heart
If only the Maker could hear my cry, I beseech him to tell
you my heart

You are truly born of beauty both within and out

Let me hold thy hand to the dancing floor
Let thy heart speak melody with softness
—and thy soul will be in perfect haven

43. Why Me

Why me .. Why me .. Why me
I thought it could be well
I thought it may had come to pass
But never did I know
Not even ever
Disappointments and hurts just
Climbed me
I would have stopped
I should have decided
But I never knew
My dreams and aspirations were changed
My flower just dropped off my hands
Why .. Why .. Why me

The crickets laughed as they danced around me in harmony

What could be the song of the flute?
As I heard same words from them
Why ... Why ... Why

Trying resolutions never worked
My flower bade me with agony
From my presence
My anxiety have proved me wrong
I should have loved my light
More than could
I should have ...

*If only the lad had gone on the desert to send the message
from the women washing in the well. It would have been a
different story
But no, the remorse of joy still is..*

*Why me .. Why me ..
Oh Creator why just me
Left desolated in this wilderness
Where I can find no help*

44. Streams Of Hurt

I walked through the garden
What a beautiful sunflower
At my surprise
She touched me from behind
She kissed me on the lips
And handed it over to me
In this light day of joy

Back home I strutted with joy
How pleasant it is to fall in love
Oh dear, my darling, I missed you

Then we saw from afar on the mountain
The burning desire as the fire sparked
It was the animal being slaughtered again as he walked
around the fire
I run happily towards her
Suddenly she lifted up his hands and said :
Woe betides you if you come further
Oh nature where did I go wrong

She denied me after all those moments
She has seen a new moon to be attached to
"You have hurt me, you have broken my heart"
I screamed at her with pain
I laid in bed with my dimed face and
My natural force abated
What a world of disappointment

I was despised, she threw me away
Deep into the blazing fire

As my body turned into ashes
My bones were still alive and it whispered to her:
I do love you and still do
Moments, conditions and pains will not just permit me
But I always wonder 'why did the tiger target its prey on the
little crow which was flying happily

45. Tears

Sobbing all day long was never the answer
Keeping awake all night never made it
Strolling away to a quiet place was the worse
Isolating from friends was not the solution

I had wanted and desired to be a virgin
But why made I a mistake
My moments of labour would soon come
I am poor and wretched
My hut was burnt because I broke tradition
She was banished from Mbata

My parents are already resting in peace
I was thrown in the thick
When the happy couple took me
They had hope!
Because they had seen their desire

But I slipped, I disappointed all eyes
Here I am again
Carrying my pot to the river side
The gods will soon be pacified

After months of labour
My baby was sacrificed to the gods
What again!
My world had never been peace

How could they been that ruthless
Is the bearing of a soul carried only a damsel?
Is the bearing of a spirit carried by what nature determines
as the right channel for offspring's?

I should have made those in the white and blue apparels
change me into a damsel

46. Had I Known

Can you judge your own wrong?
Mistakes are not always notice
Until it had pass
When I cast my mind
My conscience and my heart . . .
Then I remember those days

I vowed, I promised, I pledged
Never to repeat that mistake
I cried
I wept
I mourn
But still then
I continued, though I kept repenting

I want to quit
I have to quit
Who can reach out to me?

The aroma alone was like heaven to me
It quenched the thirst in my soul
As I gained more wisdom in my world
They cheered up praising me in high esteem as it flew away
like the vapour

If I could only tell the aftermath
I cannot tell what decision I may have taken whether of
good report or bad

I looked through the window and all I could see were noises
of different kinds
Of the birds, of the leaves, of the streams, of children, of cars
and of the wind

Suddenly I heard that noise of the lads talking about that old
leaves I never let go off in my youthful days
If only I could reach out to them, but nay the bed held me
down until eternity in my dark world

47. The Desire

Anytime the heart decides
Who can stop it?
I heard of desires
But I never knew of it
Not until I fell into it

It was so wonderful
That desire I used to have
Was critically disconnected
Was it an intruder?
No never

It was by my own self
Numerous eyes
Uncountable ears
Unfaithful mouths
Evil entities . . . .

They all made me remorse

Why should I desire for that..

It was indeed wonderful
Those days makes me joyful

But then, I couldn't stand the world
Here I find myself a preacher of it
Known in the province as the preacher

That desire, I wish I never saw or tasted
It was sweet and sour like bitter honey
Those same eyes, the same ears, and the unfaithful mouths
sat and watched me in amazement as I kept preaching

Suddenly I lost it all
What was the desire, I asked the crowd
No one could tell of the story within

That was a miracle
I was in tattered clothing
How it came, I knew not

48. When Again

I had always dreamt for a moment like this
We have been together
For days, months and years
I mean for seconds, minutes, hours and periods
I just dreamt of her touching me
We have walked for miles being mute

Until that day, she held my waist
What a strange feeling from within
I had always dreamt for such moments
Waiting and longing for that day

I felt the cold and lovely finger—round my lips

After that day, we never met like that again
Why allow the rain to part apart
When again
Shall we enjoy the dance of the women?

I am waiting for that day
On that day, for once I will . . . .

I will sing of a melody never sang before
I will sing of a hymn not ever known
I will sing like the bird and fly away

49. Though I Hate 'Ui Can't

Fowls indeed can be unfaithful
But, I never knew she could be
After all the perils
After all the troubles and pains
She fled from me

You rejected me after all those days
I thought you do love me
Anytime I get hold of you
I feel like murdering you
But when I look straight into your eyes
I fall in love again with you

Millions of you have worried me
But I still do say
You are the one I love
You saw me in the Eden
You really saw it the garden
You were and the only Eve that looked and felt it
But here am I, you stabbed at my back
I promise you, I will revenge one day

Those were the words as she lay by me
Like a sheep she looked but it was an elephant living in a tiger

You rejected me after all those days—
I said again to myself
Then I took that sharp tool that looked like a diamond
So peaceful, she looked in her paradise

THE MYSTERIES OF A VIRGIN'S AGONY

Breathless she was as I saw her in my world
Then into her heart, I pierced it with love but saw no blood

Suddenly the lights came on me
From the pit, they took me out
He is a lunatic, they all hooted at me
Poor souls I said to myself
Their days are numbered

50. Can You

As I stand
I see the weak mortals
Being brought down and buried to their homes
It makes me remember the past

See the round eyes and the lips of the red
When the moon gives it light
Then all glaze to see
When the pink long cloth was on her

The priest said,
You can now exchange biologically with her,—Weird I said
to myself
I put the ring on her finger
As we entered the new land, she slept on me forever

I went into the unseen world
My eyes opened after a decade
Then all I remember is Donna

Why do this to Daniel—her voice shivered from within
All I could do was forgive her soul

I cannot stop thinking about the past
I kept repeating those words to myself

Abruptly I saw myself being help to sit
Who could that be, I got scared
She had been my soul taker all these while when I travelled
to the unseen world
That was Donna
Confuse and scared as the air roared in the room towards me
I was dumbfounded

Was it a dream or it was real, I could not tell. Peter she said
to me, your medicine is ready
More confused I lay I decided to let go

51. Trance

It is just like the sea
When you are drowned inside
That is your end

They say I am green horn
For fifteen and eight I was
Everybody was surprise at me
They just wondered—does she know life

Then one day for the first time
I knew it
I fell in love strongly
After that night, I realised he is of stroke

Gush, I did not see that
I fell into it blindly
After being alone for those years
When I rejected all the great ones

Now here am I
In the bosom of the hospital forever
It was like a trance
But real

52. Do You Realise

I revered you so much
I respected you so much
Do you know how I thought about you?
Why can't you just give me a moment?
When you need me, I am always there for you
But when I need you
You just reject me

I wish you could read my heart
Will you ever see within it?
I love you Abigail
Who will open your eyes to see it?

Why do you treat me this way?
You mean a lot to me
I feel so isolated in the universe
I thought though the world does not recognise me
You will recognise me:
As the whole world

You are a frustration
Can't you just realise it
Sitting amongst the lads in laughter
Scorning at me as if you never knew me

As unfit as I am, I have become the damsel in your life to
serve you
I walk away in shame with little hope
That you will come home

53. Pearl

As I sat by the grave side
Tears rolled down my eyes
My eyelids have become so thick
My memories have turned to suspense

—Pearl, oh my Pearl, I think of you

Those days we did laughed together
Before that—
It was eye to eye when I met you
Then eye to lips as we chattered
It was eye to body—
Hand in hand
Hand to shoulder
Hand to waist
Then mouth to mouth

Those moments make me sad
I wish I were Ezekiel to make your dry bones to resurrect
Pearl, I love you so much
As I lay on your grave to sleep
I wish to wake no more
Not to see another day of tears
Pearl! Pearl! Pearl!
How do I continue the story when it is incomplete?

54. Why Wonder

Here she comes
All shadows ready to smile at her image
What long and dark hair
She shines as the sun and fair as the sun
And the hair as black as a cola
In her long transparent apparel
Her body looks desirable
The hour she passed by me
I stumbled as I tried to walk, but fell at all my endeavours
I tried to call her but I stammered
Tears rolled down my eyes, when I saw her go away
Just like that

As I sat down wondering
'Oh what a surprise to see you' !
I shouted:—
As she came back to where I stumbled
She held my hand
I put mine in hers

She held my shoulder, likewise I
We danced, we laughed
As we hugged each other

Then I wondered, Can the moon say to the stars—I need not
your help anymore

55. Remember

He sits lonely in the balcony
I touched him but he frowns
He is of a melancholic temperament
I tried to make him happy
I tried to make him smile
But why all these—I imagined

Remember darling, remember my love
The moments we prayed together in the river as the
crocodiles watched
The days we held each other's hands
The months we go out to celebrate
Have you forgotten so soon—

I remember the hours I spent with you at night
People gazed at us in surprise
But we still continued because I loved you

Remember my numerous letters, remember the card you gave me
But I am sorry I rejected the ring
For the future
Remember my pictures . . . . do so

Why do you make me sad, despite your health?

Despite your condition, I whispered to you
'I still do love you!
But why don't you let sleeping dogs lie
Pointing the gun at me keeps taking me into the past of good
memories
All you could do was to sniff repeatedly whilst weeping gently
Take off the weapon off my shoulder and we can sing a new
song together

56. Donna

So they say she is
No dignity can nature find in her
Despoilments are her sugar cubes
Swallowing each moment

This one is so different
The many voices shout out
Of which the human dignity
Is as of Adam

This one is different
So they say she is
Triumphantly she passes away
From town to town

No rest I find in this one
All her problems is peace to all

So they say she is
Differently, different

57. Can It Be

There are times, when I regret for my life
Certain decisions that I made makes me cry
I was blindly in love
People always talk and joy over it
When I fell into it
I did not take the right steps

Memories of the past makes me cry
My life is full of remorse
Every second is judgemental for me
I never feel comfortable
All I do is to criticise my life
Why is my life so unfair?

Some actions I took make me sob
Why did I do all these?
I could have done something else
I should have taken a firm decision
I must have learnt my lessons
But why then

I am very sorry for my life
Oh life! Is indeed a mystery
I cannot really understand my life
I was blindly in love

For how long more will I continue chanting about my remorse?
Six decades has passed us by since we had our union in our
silver years

Can it be, I asked myself each morning
Hoping there will be a change
And that change could change our world forever and we
may join the fairies soon in wonderland

58. *Bye Bye Ann*

Across the street—
When the scorching of nature became dark
For the first time we met
No sight of hers have I ever seen

She stared at me—
I glanced at her, the eye balls met
With a smile, she bid me goodbye

I crossed the street, I chased her
Horns blew at me
I turned, then bung !

On the bed, I cried
I saw the drips on me
I dreamt of her again

When the moon arose
I still thought of her
Will I ever see her again?
Never in my life had tears roll down
The doctor came near my bed in a green
apparel

Gush ! it is her again, well . . . .

59. Dissappoinment

There are moments, conditions, and periods
There are times, durations
There are hours, minutes, and seconds
There are years, months, weeks and days
When you fell so lonely

When everybody turns busy
No one ready to listen to you
It looks bleak

Can somebody just imagine?
The great pain in your heart
If only the heart was like a media
All will mourn with me

Is there nobody to listen to my tears?
Why should all turn against me?
My heart is soft and full of pain

Bitterness and hurt have eaten me up
Who will bear to hear the groaning?
Of the heart of one weeping
Well, no one cares for me

Standing on the street with my 'calabash
Passers just spat and tease
Because I was once a terror to their souls in those political times

60. Entertainment

The lights blooms off and on
To the right, to the left
Behind, round up and down
They move

He has warn me never to be there
For my first time was there
Bottles were seen everywhere
In the atmosphere, the hands, the grounds everywhere

Then bang! That life was taken good and forever . . . .

61. You Took My Life

All that I say now is goodbye
I will never forget you
You took my pain
And laid on your heart
I will never forget your love

Everyone turns against me
My hope was on people around me
I thought you were an alien
I never thought of you
I have never tried sharing my heart
With a stranger

But before I approached—
You took my life
Your concern for me was so much

Why should I be ungrateful to you?

You took my grief
And carried my bitterness

You bore them all
All that I say is—
I am grateful
But I cannot leave the room without making both of you go
to your world
My bed, you both have defiled

I am sorry to say, I am grateful but I must do this . . .

62. Tears On My Pillow

Nothing I see makes me happy
What people do never made me smile
All day and night
I laid in my bed
Rivers flew from her eyes

Sometimes I imagine how it will be like
Holding hands at the seashore
Moving to and fro
No one wishing to come near
All around me is scares and bruises

I used to be so pretty
Men revenge against each other because of me
Then on that day
Whilst strolling to a quiet place

All I could do—was to imagine my future

It was all dark,
The moon and the birds were with the stars
Then I saw him butchering me
I slouched unconscious, and then all I heard was
—You bitch! You broke my heart—

Now here I lay, no more to move

63. Before You Choose Me

All shuns me when I pass
They say I am a green horn
I swore to myself
Never ever to allow it anymore
Into my courageous heart

What a huffily young man—
Walking like a horse with power
I feared when I see you coming
My heart trembled at the sound of your voice
My feet dashed off at the noise of your footsteps

I was overwhelmed and in awe
When you chose me
I just can't say yes
All that I have been thinking of is—

What did he see before he chose me—?

Your reasons seem so many
But I have not yet heard my reason

This four beautiful lettered apple is what
I am longing to hear from you
This is my heart beat

Before I say yes

64. I Remember It

I was shock when you said it is over
I was shock when you said it is over
I never had a dream come true until I found you
What can I do to give you love
Because I will never give up

I will give you love
There is nothing in this world
I will never do

When the sun runs to a corner
I do not want to change your dream
All you need is someone to hold
I will be here for you

You need someone to trust
I am here for you
I will give you shelter

Why do you say it is over?
I will suffer my life for you
I promise
I will be there for you

Walking away will never bring you peace
Out there are clones of me
Same hands you will return if you walk away, so please don't . . .

65. *You Can Hold On Me*

Each day I live
I want to live
The best I could give
I have broken my heart
For you everyday
To taste the pain for you

You can hold on me
I want one moment of your time

I want to be the very best for your life
I have laid an opportunity
I laid a chance
I have it just for you

Give me a moment of your life
You can hold on me
Just allow me

Into your heart

I will be that angel you have longed for
I will transform into water when you are thirsty
I will transform into food when you are hungry
I will transform into a bed when you are weary
I will transform into your fairy if you find me . . . .

66. Life So Way

The self always feels complete
When the spirit groans with tears
The soul passions for them
When I hear your stories
Some are sweeter
It makes me remember
The good things in life
And the great things I did
Some are bitter
It makes me cry to curse the self
It deprives my privileges
I need some other stories
I swear
They will make me feel good
Life so way
Had no understanding
It is a mystery
The story is to see you by me
Every moment

67. *How Could That Be*

You were so cruel to me
It was very sensitive
Anytime I see your picture
Anytime I have a memory of you
It makes me remember you

Why were you so cruel to me
I used to love you
And will always be
Now that your roses ¨
Have turned green
You have rejected me

How could you be?
So that was why he chased me out?
I thought I will met you at the door

But he open the door
And you bunged up at me
You are so cruel to me
I need to take a firm decision and
Forget about you
But anytime I have a memory of you
It makes me remember you

68. If You Ask Me To

It has been a long time
I could have loved someone else
I could have trusted someone else
I just could not change my heart
I will give you my life
It only you ask me to

Since the time I have been around you
I cannot go and be someone else
If you ask me to

I will give all to you
My world is in your tongue
Speak it out
And I will do anything you want
I just cannot cross the river
Read my life
And you will know
If only you ask me to..
I will be by you

69. Not Ever

I am not for you
My heart is mine
You do not belong to my heart
When the storm subsides
Just concentrate and know—
I do not belong to you
And you don't belong to my heart

On many occasions
You turn your back on me
You carried the world

I boldly declare to you
Even as you and you, know
I do not need you, though I want you

'Baby girl! Just like that

I cannot forget you are good

This is all you say

I can't begin loving you'
It is the truth
You can't become my heart

We have been separated for years
Nothing can bring us back together
The only common thing we can have is to be always on the stage
And sing songs of our stories to the world

70. Come Home

Something special is going to happen
I have had thoughts of you
I left you sadly
When I took the wrong decision

I thought it would last for long
But it was for a moment
I have greatly missed you

When you put your hands in mine
I feel your faithfulness to me
One heart . . . . One love . . . . One mouth
Is all I give you, for the rest of my days

You say, show your trust to me
I now open up, to show my love for you
I cannot say goodbye to you
I am on my knees begging
Come home, I love you

71. Baby Girl

It has been a shame when I was lonely
For the past times of my years
I never felt this way

The first time, our eyes met
I fell in love with you
The other time I saw you
It became stronger
Now I am gone crazy
I just cannot control them

No one understands when I am joyful
I feel your mild hands round my shoulders
Speaking security to me

For a sunset when I did not see you
I nearly went mad and lunatic

My heart beats when I do not hear your voice

I have made you
The goal and desire of my heart
Never ever
Will I be sad whilst you are near

72. Show Me

It is all you have to do and say
Show me how you love me
Say how you need me
Morning and night, I feel you around

I feel so sad when you say
'I hate the way you eat'
Just show me the way you love me

I tried to make you understand
Just close your eyes
And reach your hands to me
And you will feel the touch around me
Let me walk into your open hands

I already know that you love me
Show me the way you feel
Let it be real to me
When you love me
I see the smile on your face
I fear when I lose you

I will be on a desert
You are the light of life

73. *If I*

I will have lost a great treasure
If I have not found you
Without your presence
I feel you around me

Imagine if I had not found you
You are my angel in the night
You protect me from dreams of snare

If you really want to look your best
Cast your mind into my heart
If I had to live without you
What life will I be?

You are my life, my all

Tell me now

I cannot agree without you
I cannot dream without you

There will be no second in my life
That I will forget you
If you ever leave me
You will take everything and ruin my life

74. Cry It Out

Since you came into my life
I have done anything for you to appreciate
Tell me you love me
Or walk out of my life
If you can't
Then tell me good—bye

From a distance
The world looks so gloomy to me
There is no harmony near me

The time I cry all out
Makes me feel drown in the sea
You disgraced me to the whole world
And you still keep saying
That you love me

You change my aspiration
My aims and desires were destroyed
I cannot apprehend all you did to me

Far away is hope and harmony
Just say good—bye
And I will close my heart

75. Without A Tear

Am still living with that goodbye
Am still living with the fate of misfortune
Am still living with the pain you left behind
Am still living with the rights and wrongs
Am still living with the sour and wound

I hear you are doing fine
I hear you are doing well
I hear you are happy in your state
I hear you are a hope for them
I hear you are proud to let go

You walked into my shadow Natalia
You walked into my soul
You walked into my heart with pride
You walked through my mind
You walk away from it all

Maybe that is just the way
Maybe that is how it was meant
Maybe we were not meant to love at all
Maybe it was just for a moment
Maybe I took it too serious

76. What Is The Secret

Why are all the lads fighting over you?
Why are they bruising their hearts?
Why are they filled with so much hope?
Why can't they let it go?

What is the secret that am blinded on?
What is the secret in your beauty?
What is the secret in your eyes?
What is the secret in your tongue?

Is like we never loved at all
Is like we lived like strangers
Is like there was no commonness
Is like the moon laughed at us

You walked by me with much tears
You walked by with a hopeless smile
You walked by as if life was over
You walked by and I felt guilty

Why don't you forget about the pain?
Why don't you forget about me?
Why don't you forget the past?
Why don't you let me die?

You are a beauty in their eyes
You are a queen to many
You are the princess they beseech
You are the damsel they want

Hello my queen, let go off me
And liberate thy soul
Someone out there loves you better than I did and is wishing
to carry you to his paradise

77. I Felt It

It vibrated so much when you passed by
It echoed with a bomb when you breathed on me
The earthquake when you stood still
It blew hard as you smiled back

It tried jumping out to taste of you
It stood firm trying not to kill it self
It feared if it were true or false
It trembled as it saw into your eyes

The voice stammered as it tried to show itself to you
The tale of it shared was not same as it saw it coming nearer
It was stronger than it perceived of itself
I fell on my knee as she kowtowed to say hi to me

Stunned I became
Then she walked away with a grateful smile

Why couldn't I tell her, I hit myself?
That feeling I fought on for years
Now she came into my hands freely
But I could not utter it out and she walked away

Will that chance ever come again?
When will that moment come again?
My heart jumped again with shame
Because it couldn't say to the damsel
What it had felt all these years

78. Snow Or Ice (Nonsense Poem)

As purposed as it always goes
Let me run to the damsel's house, he told himself
Although windy, cold, with severe ice falling from above, he
continued the journey
As he sat in the wheels house, he smiled to them that sat
behind him, saying in his head:—
My bosom I will satisfy again
As he sat in the wheels house, he started calculating the
quantity of intake
He kept day dreaming, that he forgot the stop

Damn, he hit his head, whilst he waited for the next wheel
Then he climbed into it, this time with full vigour in the
vision

Finally, he arrived at the maiden's abode
As planned as he always has, was waiting patiently
Just staring at the pictures whilst she went in the oven to
make haste for the intake

Finally, it was served, and he made merry and got satisfied.
Then he said to her just to prepare the platform for another
day—:
Thy intake is of quality, and in a child look tone he said,
THANK YOU with a face as of one who had never talked

The other day arrived once more
And he made haste again,
Bling bling bling bling bling
The telephone rang—

'I am gonna pass by he said to the damsel'
Great the reply came.
Busy doing the professional duty known in Europe, he heard
the beep of a message
'Pass by the cricket's home; get a petrol, matches, container
and papers for the intake you are expecting'

Oh, he said to himself when he read it
All turn to look at him in amazement
Then he said to himself
'So just this little intake, I have to travel under the sun to get these'

In haste he went for them and walked over the windy ice
and brought them with that innocent face with a burning
Stomach dying to get it filled

Then she made the intake for him
Again, with the obvious reply
'Thy intake is the best'
She looked at him as if to pierce his eyes with a rod, and said
to herself
'U dey craze?

As he prepared to leave, the damsel gave him his travelling
bag with the remaining of the intake and he said as if he was
in burning desire to give up Hades for a paradise
'Oh no, I do not need it, please keep it, for I return to finish it
up another day'
But she insisted and said no, take thy trouble with thee

As he got out of the maiden's house, he turn to look at her
door with an evil eye as to burn the whole community and
said to himself
'You think I was gonna leave the rest for you, next time tell
me to go buy ingredients for my intake'

79. *The Dream*

And the singers ceased singing because I had come to a standstill

As I watched from afar
True love is what I had fathom from her womb

As I remembered those days,
It was true love I saw from deep her eyes

As I watched her, talk from her lips,
It was true love I could hear her sing to my soul

Whence I find this to embrace, became a melody of no lyrics
Whence I find this to lie on, became an instrument of no play
Whence I find this to soothe my pain, was of no pillow to lie on

As I lay on my bed

They became frequent battles I had no sword to fight on
When will that day come, was a question I found no answer for

But of one song I can sing in my heart
And of that song, my soul will get revitalised
Because that day shall come soon with its glory
My sunshine I will see each morning
In her bosom, I will feel secure

On that day, we shall walk side by side
On the day she will walk to me and I will welcome her with love
On that day, I will unveil her to the world
On that day, I will announce to the world, she is my pride

And to my first safe home, I will go to seek blessings
Unto her, I will say, say unto me the blessings you wish for me
And those words I know shall be the act of my beloved

As I lay to sleep, I wake soon on that day and I will see her
in the pew
And love, shall be the lyrics of the new song for the dancers

80. Weaker & Weaker

Just as I said, here I am
Just as you asked, here I am

The wound you promised to heal
The wound you promise to wake

Seeing you today was my desire
Seeing you yesterday was as I wished

The bruise I showed to you
The bruise I brought forth

You looked deep into the wound
You looked deep into the bruise

That was the dark days
That was the past days

The wound was healed as I recall
The wound was no more as I evoke

Was in awe when I saw it was new
Was in shock when I realised this

You dug into the wound
You dug into the bruise

Why did you make it strong?
Why did you make it look true?

THE MYSTERIES OF A VIRGIN'S AGONY

If it was for a season
If it was for a period

Please explain why you open it
Please explain why you dug into it

That was a healing wound
That was a scare healed of a wound

Why did you open that scare?
Why did you put fire in it?

Why did you make it strong?
Why did you make it brawny?

Did you know you were the healer?
Did you know you healed and tore it?

81. Before I Fall Deeper

She gave me all the smiles I needed
She gave me all the comfort one could wish for
She made me feel like I have never felt before
She made me see the world differently
She brought a lost desert on my land

My racing heart has never been the same
I love to say I do if she only asks for it
I love to say I will if she only adheres
My racing heart shall be same always

Seeing her from a distance makes me complete as I had
always dreamt
Seeing her in those apparels as she becomes the chef during
the hours, makes me feel on top of the world

But hey, my spirit became calm although aggressive
My spirit got sour although sweet
My spirit danced with her although with hatred
My spirit felt like a looser although the promoter
It had better leave right now
She was all my offspring wanted
She was all my own could wish for
How could I make her my own was a million question to be
answered

As she walk in the pew with me
All I could imagine was 'I 'waiting
As I walk in the pew with her
All she could imagine was a loving father to be

My racing heart gets faster and faster
As we approach the standpoint of my own, flesh and blood
As I look into his eyes, I see innocence and fear as to come to
my abode for shelter and comfort

If he knew, how I felt for his beloved
I will have become his enemy forever
But here I am with an open arm of love to direct his every step

What could be the cause in my heart?
It became so, as she looked like my departed heart I once
could sing with
My departed heart that bore my offspring's for me

82. On The Stage

That was the dream as we sang together
Saying to the many to hold on tight and never let go
Filling into the heart of many to tell them of true union

Do you ever realise what this does to me
Every day as I sing with you
Every day as I walk with you
Every day as I learn with you
Every day as I practice with you

Looking deep into your eyes
Looking deep unto those lips
Looking deep into those eye balls

Makes me want to have you forever
Singing with you on that table makes me
Feel I have you forever
Singing with you in front of them makes me feel like am in
wonderland

I do not want to let go
I do not want to lose the moments
I do not want to see it for a while
I do not want to walk away anymore

Let us continue the story after the stage
Let us continue to hold our hands
Let us continue the songs until the end
Let us not stop the melody we created

But just as time flies, the music ended
And the players finished their parts

As we walked away to our various ways
I was dreaming you would walk back
Praying and hoping you will be mine
Wishing to be in your arms baby

As I watched the moon getting smaller
And fading away, same as you walked off

That dream of mine never came to pass
We were meant for just the stage
If I could only have you in my arms there
I could only hear your heart beats from the stage and it
fades after that

I gave you my world on the stage
But to you it was just for a show
How sad it is that you can't read my lips

83. She Found It

Love as it is known is difficult to explain
Sometimes you think you are in love already
Only to find your own lover out of no where
It makes you feel like you want to shoot your heart out

Loving the person so dear to you is like admiring nature's beauty
She never dreamt of falling in love this deep, ever
But, it came so quickly & out of no where
He has taken her heart completely
And it makes her feel like the path to it has been cleared off
She just cannot fathom or trace the path that led to it
She thought they would never be anything beyond friends

Love is so difficult to explain as the author defines . . . .
Heaven stands for those who stand for true love
In a special way to keep them forever
'My baby, remain my sugar forever in my sore life'
I want to be closer to you, everyday
Your love will make me brighter everyday

Memories of our old year's cannot be remembered by our
honesty
She never thought they could go beyond friendship
Even when they have not met for year
The gravity seems to bring her more closely than she
imagines

Closer than she can be to you
It's so nice, so nice, so sweet, so nice
Its just sad she doesn't know when she will see you
But Alas, she is happy she found her heart in you

84. Untold Story

That was all about the untold story that faded off
Hitherto the dame seemed lost in the fairy tale
As the hours passed by, it suggested mitigating critcism

Back to the days the memory strutted
Was it in an ostentatious way, who could tell

Alas, she created a world of two from unknown histories
What she was to meet was of fear & doubt without faith
Finally the strange figures came into contact

Why did I come, she asked herself
I had no need of a blanket though I need a comforter
She said in her mind, that gonna be the last to see him

Unplanned but the souls had their own purposes who could see
With curiosity & a feeling without explanation they met again
Off on the street they walked like friends known for long

Beautiful :as the leaves whispered to each other,they walked on
That sugar ice with the brown colour & flavor was amazing

Ahoy! Ahoy! Ahoy! A voice yelled from afar, but none
heared
It all looked beautiful with sparkling golf all around
How wonderful were those moments of a friendship with no rope

Oh, that scene alway amazes me when I walk on that path
Loosing a new friend becuase he felt I had found my true path
I saw him today, all he could do was pretend I had not
surface

The breeze spoke so deep but I heard not that saw them swim
That was the best afternoon, I could have ever wished for
How tremendous, that moment will never elapsed

Oh that massage, took me to Mary in wonderland
As I beheld the elfves & fairies on a chronological pace
Everything sequenced like an untold story

A good friend I found who could have thought of
Of the Suomi Land, had never given a thought to it
But it just happened, without purposeful ly planning

How do I narrate to my old friend, was a continuous battle
Whatever the situation, that will be my pocket dictionary till...

That story ended with no conclusion & full of confusion

85. *The Night*

The night is lonely without you
Its like walking in the night and finding your star to be with
Knowing very well that it is hard to come by that star
The stars above are uncountalbe with different glows

Walking alone in the night makes me feel my love feels same
But walking in the night with my love happy makes me
happy as well
Loving him has been a story of the untold
It was like finding the lost coin I never dreamnt of

My heart beats at every sound of the coin
As it keeps bouncing up and down without resting
Though the night has been less with the presence of the coin
bouncing
I kept smiling because I have too many coins to keep
counting

Counting them never got me weary
At every coin I pick, i just smiled as I read with esctacy
Without expectancy, a coin just dropped and my heart
dropped as well
Picking it up and reading got me more excited

I cant seem to stop saying, 'I luv you' as I keep reading
Loving you has been like a good curse on the land of Canann
Everything looks so saccharine and I hope it doesnt become bitter
Staring continuosly at his image make me want to see him in
person

Saying i love you continuoly means so much to me
I have no explanations to what i feel wthin
But all I know is, your heart is safe with mine and I will
always love you
If loving you is all you will ever wish for then am 'gonna'
love you forever
If keeping you in my heart is what you have longed for, I
will gladly bury it there
If kissing you all day is what will keep you strong, then my
lips will draw all over you
If hugging you is all you dream of, I will always hug you to sleep
If chatting with you makes you happy, then am all yours
forever

All I want is to be with you and stay in your arms forever
All I desire, is to lie on your hairy chest like a babe wanting milk
All I ever hope for is to play with thy bear and tell u how
much I luv you
All I dream of is to see your every smile everyday to give me hope
All I pray for is for you to cherish me as you never ever did
to any woma

Your tender love rekindles my burning & overwhelming love
First time we 'gonna' meet, we 'gonna' have same feelings
The fire in us will always be turned on
Do not feel lonely my love
You are all I ever want & never prayed for
So please wait a little bit longer until we meet

Forgive me, because am so much in love with you
Do not dream to deny me because am painfully in love
I feel like this is the best time of love am sharing
I feel am getting closer to you every time and it seems un
enough

I wish I could remember the smell of your skin
I wish I could remember any love story we ever had
Nevertheless, we never did, but will soon have it in reality
You are the only one I will continually love
So please wait for our love and never give up
Forgive me; I do not know what is happening
But am so much in love and not ready to give up
I need you more than I can ever hope for
Forgive me, because I won't cease to love you

86. The Music

The music fainted & passed out like the flame that candled
the dark room
The dance floor was empty although the players stood by
their instruments
The heart of the dancers were lost only to be found under the
stage melting off
The lyrics to the fairy song was left hanging on the dry leaf
outside the room
I entered the room ready to dance only to find it was a dead
cemetery . . . .

87. The Cross

Then I run out of the room and all I saw was the woods
Flocks of all kinds of human, animals, birds and so on
crowded
They were all looking up to one thing and it was a scroll
The scroll was displayed & the crowd struggled to read
From behind, I run through, fighting to read what it said
As I saw, my name signed underneath the notes from afar
I reached there & a heard a fainting voice call my name,
I turned back for a minute then turn again to read the scroll
Only to find it burning & the last word I saw was
Cecilia] . . . .
On top of it was someone nailed on the cross & bleeding
I yelled out with pain to ask what sin was committed
Only to realise i was all along deaf & dumb . . .
All I could do was to watch as the dying soul bleeds to
death . . .

Your Diary / Personal pages

Your Diary / Personal pages

Your Diary / Personal pages

Other Books Written By The Author

'MY DIARY POETRY OF HOPE, DESPAIR
& FREEDOM'
(Motivational, Emancipation & Educational)

About the Author

She is multi— talented and does best what she loves doing. She is a passionate woman who has the flair of putting what she sees, feels and experiences, hears and understands in the form of poetry in a very way that appeals to the senses of the audience in a passionate and natural manner. Poetry has been her passion and life from her early teens. Cecilia Naa Densua Quarshie is very articulate, creative and a good team player as well as a good motivator. She has worked with different International Organizations such as the Planned Parenthood Association of Ghana, African Youth Alliance, Pathfinder International, Christian Health Association of Ghana, Academy for Education and Development, Doscar Travel & Tours and many others for 7 years in Ghana before relocating to Finland to further her studies. She has worked in the areas of a Research Assistant, Counselor, Ticket Sales Assistant, Peer Educator, Secretary and a Public speaker.

In Finland, she has a hobby job apart from her normal work as a Performance Poet & a Singer. It is her passionate wish that readers enjoy reading her poems and relate it to real life situations.

About the Book

This book is intended for all purposes, which includes classroom discussion on poetry and other purposes such as performing poetry, readers own pleasure and so on. Most of the poems have real story lines in them, which are very emotional and should be read as such.

For classroom purposes such as discussions, the writer uses a number of literary terms such as simile, metaphors, irony and in some parts keeps the reader in suspense. Some of the poems are clear and straightforward whereas others are not straightforward. Some get the interest of the reader going as this keeps the reader in suspense and anxious for what follows next.
It is the writers hope that all readers make good use of the book in their own unique way.